WITHDRAWN

4/08

How to Draw

Watercraft

For Jesse, Jasmine, Justin, Jordan, Melina, and Matthew

Published in the United States of America by The Child's World®
1980 Lookout Drive • Mankato, MN 56003-1705
800-599-READ • www.childsworld.com

Acknowledgments
Illustration and Design: Rob Court
Production: The Creative Spark, San Juan Capistrano, CA

Library of Congress Cataloging-in-Publication Data
Court, Rob, 1956–
  How to draw watercraft / by Rob Court.
    p. cm. — (Doodle books)
  ISBN 978-1-59296-958-6 (library bound : alk. paper)
 1. Boats and boating in art—Juvenile literature. 2. Drawing—Technique—Juvenile literature. I. Title. II. Series.

NC825.B6C68 2008
743'.8962382—dc22

2007013396

The Scribbles Institute ™

Doodle BOOKS ™

How to Draw

Watercraft

by Rob Court

The Child's World®

rowboat

1

2

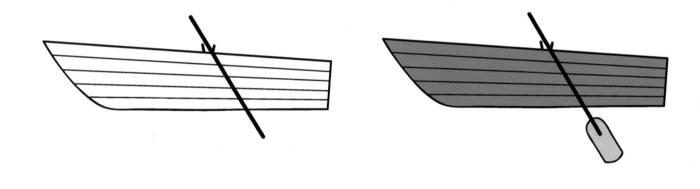

3

4

sailboat

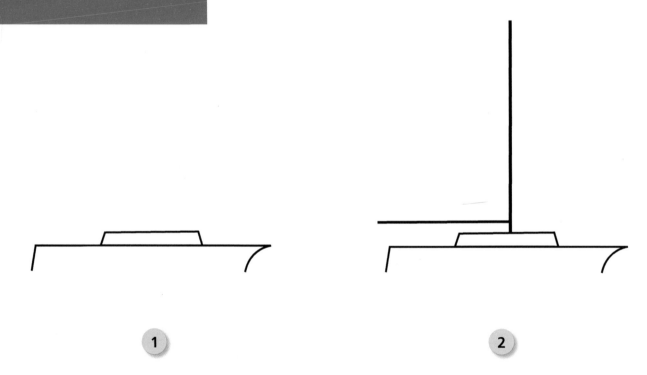

1

2

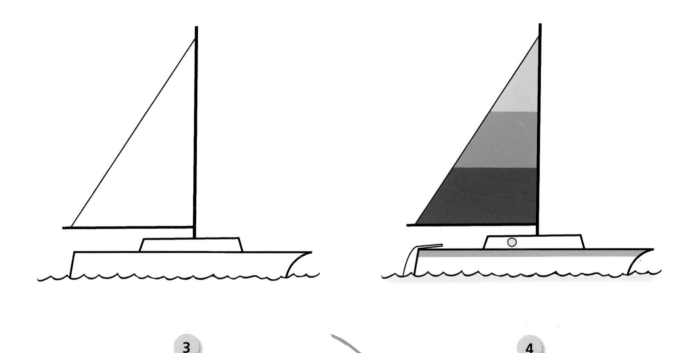

3

4

motorboat

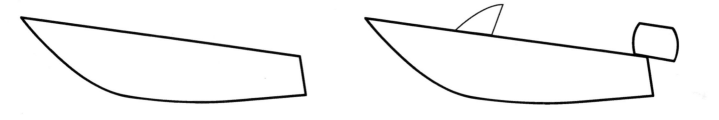

1

2

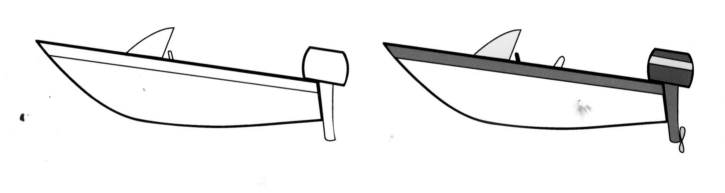

3

4

raft

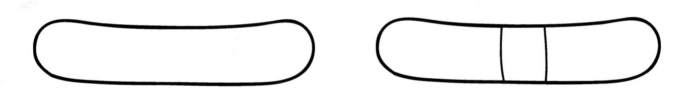

1

2

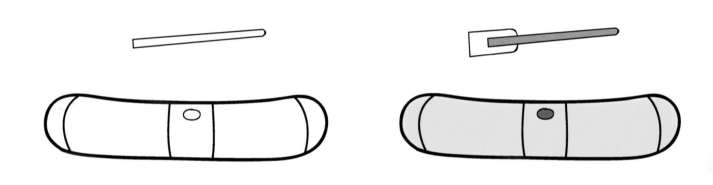

3

4

pontoon

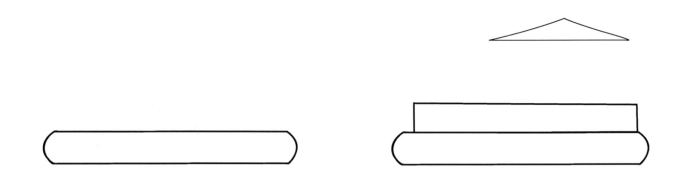

1

2

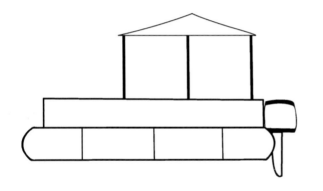

3

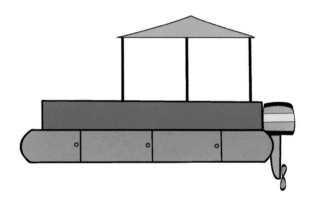

4

personal watercraft

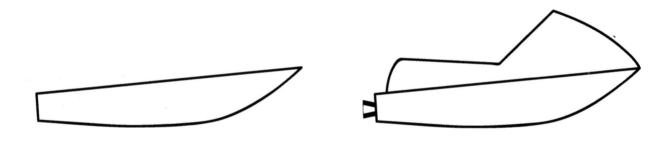

1

2

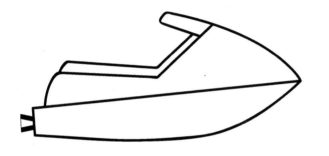

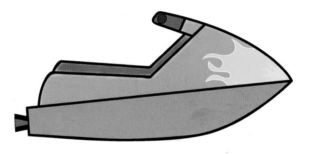

3

4

tugboat

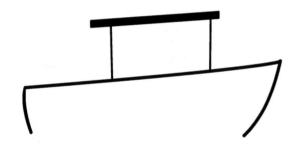

1

2

3

4

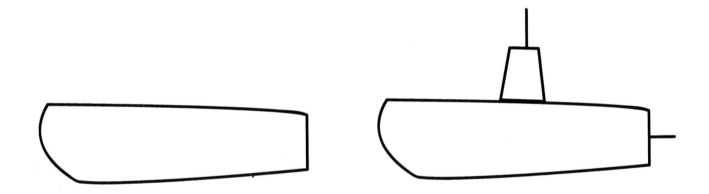

1

2

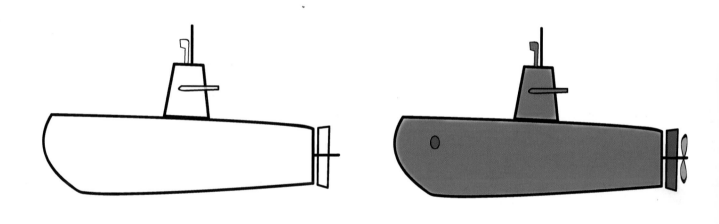

3

4

yacht

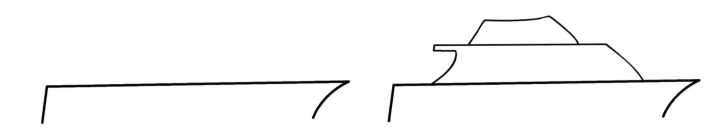

1

2

3

4

barge

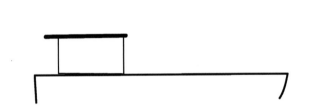

1

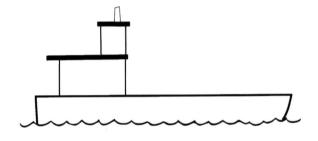

2

3

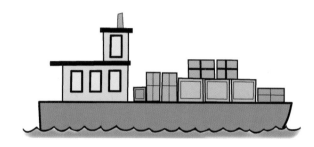

4

canoe

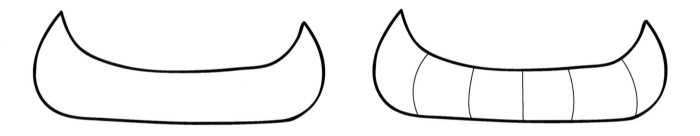

1

2

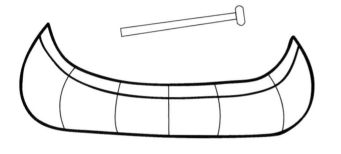

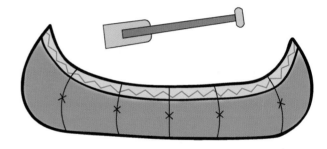

3

4

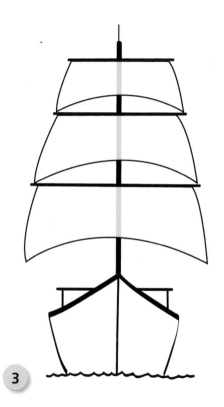

3

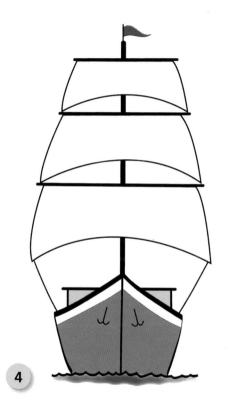

4

kayak

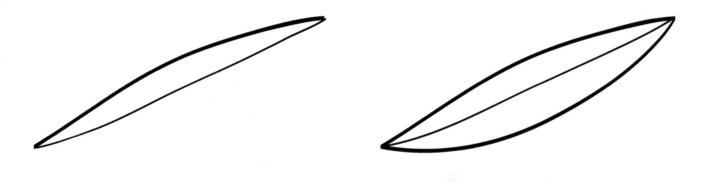

1

2

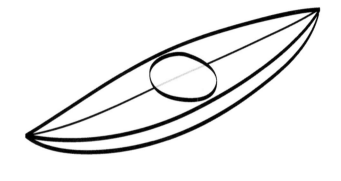

3

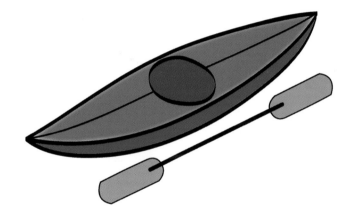

4

catamaran

1

2

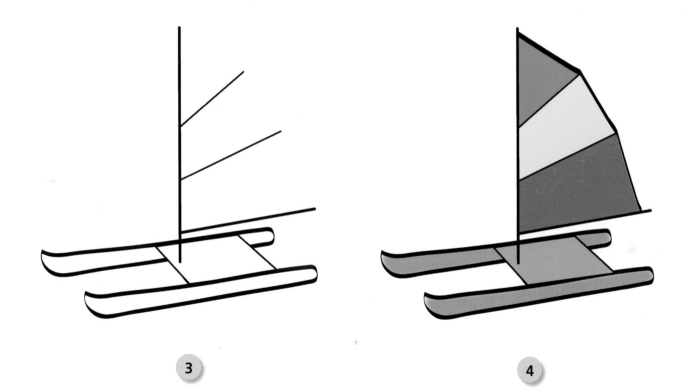

3

4

lines

horizontal

vertical

angled

curved

thick

thin

dotted

squiggly

dashed

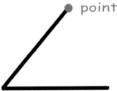 point

Move a point to make a line.

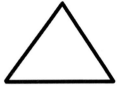

Connect lines to make a shape.

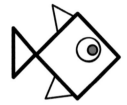

Shapes make all kinds of wonderful things!

loop

Repeating dots, lines, and shapes makes patterns.

About the Author

Rob Court is a graphic artist and illustrator. He started the Scribbles Institute to help students, parents, and teachers learn about drawing and visual art. Please visit www.scribblesinstitute.com